30 Useful Marketing Tips for Selling Your Home

By

Dorothy Ahlswede, J.D., DVM

Dedication

This book is dedicated to the memory of my mother, Mary Elizabeth McKenzie. She worked for many years as an R.N. and also for a briefer period of time as a real estate sales agent. She was the kindest person I ever met, a true inspiration.

Introduction

Do you plan to place your residence on the real estate market soon? If so, you can sometimes enhance your ability to obtain offers by taking a few simple steps to make your property more attractive to buyers. Exceptions always exist, of course, but for the most part people selling real estate can often help a home "show" much better by following a few simple guidelines. These steps do not need to cost you a lot of money. Best of all, undertaken in the right frame of mind, getting a home ready for the market can even involve some fun!

My Story

I am an attorney and veterinarian licensed in Colorado. While attending a veterinary program in a lovely Front Range community in the Centennial State, I obtained a real estate sales license and worked in partnership with my mother selling residential property as sales associates of Wheeler Realty in Fort Collins. Our broker, Bill Neal, possessed extensive experience in the real estate industry. Mr. Neal and his wife, Carol, worked together in both real estate sales and commercial development. They assisted clients with complex real estate issues. They also supported the local community and the real estate profession with great dedication.

Wheeler Real Estate in Fort Collins was an exceedingly happy place to work. The firm maintained a vibrant, enthusiastic and friendly office with a high morale. Sales associates helped one another. My mother and I were fortunate to receive considerable kind assistance and training from some outstanding brokers and experienced sales professionals. I enjoyed the opportunity to attend many, many open houses and to observe the marketing campaigns developed for a variety of residential properties very closely.

While I cannot say that I possess extensive experience as a real estate salesperson, some issues did impress me in terms of simple measures that can (and probably should) be take by home owners who decide to place their residential properties on the market. Frequently following just a few basic principles can greatly enhance the market viability of properties.

Today, some locations around the nation do not enjoy the benefit of ready access to professional real estate services. Home owners, especially those in rural areas and small towns, may struggle to prepare their properties for the sales market without the benefit of any marketing assistance from local real estate agents or brokers. Hopefully, this brief book will be able to provide a few helpful tips that people preparing properties for the market will find useful.

Chapter One: Ten General Principles

Tip #1: Try to Consider Your Home from the Perspective of a Buyer

This first point will probably sound _so obvious_ that many readers will dismiss the advice. Don't do that! This idea represents the most important key in marketing your property.

You love your home. After all, you made the smart decision to purchase it in the first place, right?

After residing in the property for weeks, months or years, you think of it as a welcome harbor, a place of shelter, security and grace. Your family members may have lovingly painted the hallways, selected furnishings and conducted regular garage sales in the front yard. Maybe you invest time cleaning out the gutters every year, raking leaves, mowing the lawn and performing a variety of other regular maintenance tasks around the premises.

This mindset suits home owners perfectly. Yet when the time comes to place your family's lovely home on the real estate market, it remains **imperative** to view it through the eyes of a buyer. In fact, it even helps to take a somewhat critical point of view.

In order to make the premises as attractive as possible to prospective purchasers to expedite sales offers you must look at the entire property with a high degree of detachment. This assignment can drain you emotionally. It's difficult.

Objectivity remains one of the primary reasons why some sellers find retaining a real estate sales professional **much** easier than preparing their own property for the market. Some of the tips that follow will perhaps prove distressing, unless you can first mentally and emotionally distance yourself a little bit from your home.

Contemplating the sale of a dwelling you have labored over, a structure that housed your family and contributed happy moments to their lives, to some extent resembles embarking on an organized, protracted grieving process. In order to send a residence to the market, it's next lifetime in a sense, it remains necessary to say good-bye mentally first.

One way to begin this difficult process involves a terminology change. Try to refer to your residence during conversations as "this house" or "this property" and not as "our home."

Tip #2: Your Possessions= Some One Else's Clutter

The corollary to tip number one involves removing as many items of your family's personal property from the premises as possible. Most real estate agents agree that properties with minimal furnishings sell much faster.

What accounts for this?

Possibly the presence of another family's belongings everywhere makes it much harder for a prospective buyer to visualize his or her household residing on the premises. When you walk into a room and see someone else's tennis shoes sitting on the floor in the closet and their books and trophies lining the shelves of the den, imaging yourself living in the same location seems a bigger leap somehow.

Sellers should do everything within their power to facilitate a potential buyer's ability to envision a "sold" sign in the front yard. This means un-cluttering counters, drawers and bathroom shelves, cleaning out closets, and sending athletic equipment, shop tools, family heirlooms and children's toys into temporary storage. You can re-arrange all these items in their correct place once you move into your new home in another location.

Converting to a minimalist lifestyle, at least for the duration of time that your residence remains on the real estate market, in some cases may prove to be _the single most important step_ that you as a property owner can take to expedite a sale.

This phase of the relocation process also proves one of the most difficult for families. It can require great self-discipline to function with a bare minimum of personal items nearby, especially if you have become comfortably well entrenched in a residence over the course of decades.

There is a joke about a couple whose friend politely inquired if they had sold their house yet? One of them replied: "We've decided not to after watching our real estate agent's on line video about the home. It was just the place we were looking for!"

So just focus instead on the joy you will experience when your property closes quickly. Be ruthless with yourself.

If there is a question about whether the plastic flowers on the patio should go or stay, remove them. Always err on the site of reducing your personal belongings from the house prior to placing it on the market. Box, label, store, sell and move on.

Tip #3: Location, Location, Location

There is a (very) old real estate sales maxim. You can turn it to your advantage when the time arrives to place your residential property up for sale.

"What *really* sells property?"

"Location. Location. Location."

This idea seems rooted in the notion that particular one-of-a-kind settings will always enjoy popularity as dwelling locations, because no one can reproduce them. The incredible beauty of the Rocky Mountains, the wonderful sandy beaches of Florida or the vivid, lovely landscape of Vermont's hillsides during autumn...Who can place a price tag on those scenes? Apartment units located close to commercial centers in many urban areas command high prices; everyone wants to live in proximity to certain places.

Even if you don't reside in a high-demand spot, there are still many wonderful aspects about your home that many people would appreciate. And your real estate remains unique. No one else can ever really reproduce it.

When a professional real estate sales person considers marketing real estate, one of the first steps that person will take involves getting out a map and studying it closely. For experienced agents with many clients, the map became a purely mental exercise years ago.

Yes, most successful realtors do know local neighborhoods just *that* well.

In order to market properties, real estate agents and brokers spend hours of time driving along streets in the locale. Many have walked through the neighborhood multiple times, also. They develop a visceral understanding for the styles and types of houses located there. They know the general price ranges, the quality of the nearby schools and the number of large employers within five miles. They can tell you what houses of worship serve the local population, the size of the closest mall and the types of transportation issues residents faced last year due to weather conditions.

Possibly you have resided in your home for 45 years, and regurgitating that type of information to a total stranger on short notice would prove challenging? Don't feel bad. You spent time *living* in your neighborhood. Local real estate sales professionals have *studied* it.

But when you do decide to market your home, a good early tactic involves stepping back and taking a long, hard look at your local environment. If you have not already done so, ask yourself some questions:

- How has the neighborhood changed during the past five years?
- What are the best aspects of living in this location?
- Are there any unattractive issues, e.g. a recent crime problem or gradually developing roadway congestion or pets roaming unleashed in the area or noisy parties on the weekend?
- Do I know the names of my neighbors on this block? Where do they work and what kind of local neighborhood social events do we all attend every year?
- What are residential properties on this street worth today?

- Where is the nearest grocery store? Police department? Medical facility? Cinema? Park?
- Who is my local city council person, my mayor, my school board representative, my congressional representative?
- Why is it better to reside in my house than one six miles across town?
- Why am I selling my property and moving away from this neighborhood at this time?

It can help to obtain a personal notebook and write all the information you gather about your location down in a single place. Later, when your house goes on the market, your notes will provide an invaluable resource to use in developing sales strategies and materials.

Tip #4: An Honest Self-Assessment

Don't overlook the importance of evaluating your particular property as objectively as possible. Just as you must pay attention to its location, consider all of the features of the home with a critical eye. Pretend that you are considering buying it for the first time. What would you tell yourself about the residence now?

Take another section in your notebook to list features about your house. Note some important information that buyers will want to know:

- The number and sizes of the rooms and closets;
- The specific number of bathrooms and all their features;
- The age of the house;
- The size and condition of basements and attics;

- Energy saving features in the residence;
- The size of the yard or common area and its amenities;
- The size and features of the garage, if any;
- The types of utility systems and the names of providers;
- Your monthly utility bills for the past year;
- The type of roof covering the residence;
- The date the roof was most recently replaced, if applicable;
- List any appliances you plan to leave on the premises;
- The date carpet was installed;
- The name of the home building company that constructed the home;
- The amount of your property taxes over the past three years;
- The amount you spend every month for television, phone and computer access;
- The cost of any homeowner association fees or condominium association fees;
- Any problems involving the property or its systems that required repairs.

You may take a lot of this type of information for granted today. But remember, someone interested in purchasing your property will not necessarily know the basics about your home. So try to help them by recording everything accurately.

It also makes sense to write down features you have enjoyed or disliked about living in your residence. If you love awakening to the sound of birds singing in the back yard, make sure you note this fact. If a passing nearby train rattles your breakfast table every weekend, record that type of information also.

Some sellers will go a step further and hire an independent qualified property inspector with prior experience in construction to examine their home and prepare a report about the findings. This precaution can help you make certain that you disclose every bit of information to prospective buyers concerning the condition of the premises. If one of your residential systems requires replacement or significant repair, such as the plumbing, heating or roof, this step can alert you to the issue in advance. It is better to know about possible problems going into a sale than to find out just before closing that a problem exists.

Tip #5: Don't Dismiss Neighborhood Trends

Just like people, neighborhoods tend to change over time. You need to recognize that these trends impact property appreciation. Sometimes the transformation leads to soaring property values and other times the opposite trend holds true.

For instance, a neighborhood in a suburb may start out as mainly residential. But over the course of a decade, if a number of small businesses begin operating at nearby intersections. The character of the locale may gradually change from residential to primarily commercial.

Homeowners sometimes receive a nasty shock when it comes time to sell. They may assume buyers would be lining up to purchase their now more heavily taxed homes. But sometimes residential neighborhoods transform into busy urban centers and buyers reject the established neighborhood in favor of newer suburbs. By carefully examining changes in your "neck of the woods" you may determine that it makes a great deal of sense to market your home for use as a potential business office rather than as a home, for example.

You may discover that if the character of your neighborhood has changed significantly, you fare better in the real estate market by entrusting your sale to a real estate professional rather than attempting to market the property yourself. My point here: **it pays to consider this type of issue in advance**. Don't miss out on thousands or hundreds of thousands of dollars because you market your property in the wrong way.

Just a few signs that a neighborhood may be changing in significant ways include:

- The presence of more businesses in the immediate area;
- Graffiti appearing on street signs, walls and other structures (where none used to exist);
- A very high percentage of homes going on the market;
- Nearby farm land turning into subdivisions;
- Gated communities going up nearby;
- A big change recently in your property taxes;
- New street assessments and nearly constant ongoing road work within a few blocks of your residence

Tip #6: Ask Questions

If you don't know the answer to a question as you study your property and your neighborhood, don't hesitate to dig more deeply into issues that spark your curiosity. You may never find an answer to your questions unless you search diligently.

There is a very old joke about a child who kept pestering his parents with questions. "Why is the sky blue? What is the dog thinking about? Will I ever meet a real dinosaur? How does a light bulb work?" He posed the wide array of fanciful inquiries that young children spend time focusing on at a certain stage of life.

In frustration, his busy father retorted: "Why are you wasting your time asking me so many silly questions, son? What would have happened if I had spent all my time as a young man doing that?"

"Maybe you would be able to answer mine now?" The child ventured.

So don't allow anyone to deter you from your quest to learn more information about your real estate in order to market it more effectively. Even questions that you fear might sound ignorant are valid if you do not know the answer. In the final analysis, learning results from questions.

Many potential sources of information on local real estate topics exist. You may find it helpful to visit your county courthouse and review public property information for your street. Additionally, neighbors may know a lot about local conditions. Don't hesitate to politely ask them to share their knowledge with you.

Another good source of local real estate information may be the public library. For example, if you don't know the names and addresses of potential large employers located close to your home, a reference librarian may help you ferret out this type of useful factual data. Your local Chamber of Commerce or Community Business Development organization will often offer assistance, as well.

Why go through this extensive effort to really learn about your neighborhood and real estate? It may ultimately support your marketing efforts.

For example, if you discover that a new company with hundreds of employees will move just a mile or so away from your home, then you might find it useful to contact the firm's Personnel Office to let them know when you place your house on the market.

Finally, don't overlook helpful on line sources of information. These resources may not always be accurate because on line information does not undergo extensive fact checking sometimes. But they can provide a good starting place for gaining preliminary information that you can later verify.

Tip #7: Imagine a Buyer Purchasing Your Home

Take a few moments when you have gathered all the data about your property and its location, and try and imagine the sale of your home. Sit quietly in a comfortable location. Envision yourself walking away from the closing table with a big check. This visualization exercise can help renew your motivation for getting the home ready for the market.

It is not possible to accurately predict who your buyer will be, of course. But evaluating the home carefully and looking at the neighborhood closely can sometimes assist your marketing efforts, helping you to tailor your preparations towards the needs purchasers.

For example, if you reside in a six bedroom home and you now plan to move to a retirement community during a downsizing effort, which type of buyer is more likely to desire your property: an elderly couple or a family with four teenagers and some foster children? I'm betting on the household with kids.

You don't want to turn anyone away, ever. Elderly buyers might surprise you. But just be aware that an inquiry from a buyer desperately in need of more space is *probably* going to be more productive in your case as you market a six bedroom home.

Trying to get a subjective sense of the likely buyers of your home can help you in preparing the property for the marketplace. It may enable you to emphasize certain attributes of the home and forget about enhancing others prior to a sale. Some sellers make a serious mistake by "over improving" their home before a sale, adding amenities that would be nice in more expensive homes but which simply make their modest house more difficult to sell for the higher price now required to break even.

It often makes more sense to sell an unimproved property at a lower price than to expend a lot of time and money adding expensive upgrades that require you to charge a higher sum in order to sell. Focusing on your potential market can help you avoid that type of pricing error.

Tip #8: Perform a House "Beautification" Analysis

So, after you have completed evaluating your neighborhood and your residence very thoroughly, in order to obtain top dollar for your property, you may find it useful to enhance your residence. Ask yourself a question:

What would most enhance the attractiveness of the residence to an imaginary buyer?

Walk through the house and grounds after finishing reading this book and note three issues with a critical eye:

1. Things requiring repair or maintenance.
2. Improvements that would make the home more attractive.
3. The estimated budget for each step.

Many people can work with only limited funds when it comes time to preparing their residence for the real estate market. This usually means that some repairs or improvements will not prove cost-effective, while others remain too simple and inexpensive to not consider implementing as soon as possible.

Perhaps you have yearned for some time to remodel the unfinished basement into a second family den? But when you examine your home, you realize that your limited home improvement and home marketing budget will get far more "bang for the buck" spending the money cleaning the roof. Now is the time to prioritize those types of hard decisions.

You may resolve after reviewing the entire house to make a few basic repairs and then work to clean and beautify the exterior. If you win the lottery next week, you can spend some of the money adding additional downstairs rooms (**if** it turns out that this step would be **cost effective** when you sell).

Many online property buyers find extremely low priced deals when they consider purchasing "fixer upper" homes advertised on line. In fact, some of these types of properties sell for the underlying value of the land alone. The asking price may be incredibly low precisely because the structure itself in damaged condition possesses essentially no value as a residential property. Buyers eventually learn the hard way that sometimes a fixer upper often does not represent a lucrative real estate investment at all. The cost of repairing a rehab property may far outweigh its value. Situations vary widely.

Tip #9: Use Your Special Skill Sets to Full Advantage

In prioritizing your repair and upgrade list, one factor may change the way you prioritize your "to do" items. If you possess special skill sets, then you may be able to enhance your property cost-effectively in a way that someone else could not.

For instance, if you are a skilled plumber, with access to wholesale supplies, you may possibly find it cost effective to re-pipe a plumbing system. Most other home owners might find the same task both daunting and expensive. Similarly, a professional electrician might consider upgrading an unfinished basement area by adding additional electrical outlets. This step would not prove cost-effective for some other owners, perhaps.

Real estate remains one field in which skilled craftsmen possess a distinct advantage. Carpenters, masons, landscapers, roofers, painters, plumbers, electricians, welders and other artisans can often discover creative ways to enhance their properties significantly before a sale using "sweat equity", without spending a lot of money on upgrades.

One of my former supervisors spent several years working in the JAG Corps before he retired as a Colonel. He possessed extensive construction experience, having spent one summer as a young man helping his older brother complete the framing of a subdivision. They built a number of houses together from the ground up that year. He also enjoyed woodworking and over the course of several years became a very talented carpenter.

He traveled extensively in the course of his military service. One method he discovered for enhancing his family's financial security involved purchasing his family residence and improving it before selling. He continued this practice after re-entering the civilian work force. I possess no military experience at all, but it is my impression that his strategy can work well for many people who face frequent employer-directed relocations, such as military service personnel or hotel and air carrier industry executives.

If someone enjoys working in a highly skilled home improvement capacity and that person has developed talents in a construction-related field, buying, improving and re-selling real estate in some cases can offer a lucrative way to offset relocation costs.

Tip #10: Documentation

For a variety of reasons, it usually makes sense to retain careful records of any home repair and improvement efforts you undertake prior to a sale. Not only will this step allow you to demonstrate property value enhancements to interested buyers, but taxing authorities may want access to the information, as well.

So try and keep a careful record of the steps you take to improve your home before a sale. This effort will help you make certain that you do not exceed your available home beautification budget. If an improvement appears likely to cost far more than you originally anticipated, you can take steps as early as possible to curtail costs.

What should you do if a repair really needs completed, but money is not available? In that situation, it may be useful to discuss your problem with your legal advisor.

Sometimes people facing difficult financial situations must sell a property, but at the same time cannot afford to correct glaring defects in the property. Possible solutions might range from offering to credit prospective buyers with a sum to offset the repairs they will be required to make after the purchase, to applying for an emergency short term "bridge loan" to pay for necessary contractor work. These situations can become complex sometimes. It remains prudent to obtain qualified professional advice if you find yourself facing that type of dilemma. It may be necessary to obtain special disclosures from everyone involved before proceeding and to notify mortgage lenders and insurance companies about some problems.

Chapter Two: Principles of Curb Appeal

Tip #11: The Concept of "Curb Appeal" Influences Buyers

People often hear real estate agents extolling the virtues of "curb appeal." This expression in real estate-speak remains a bit flirtatious. It's like a man casually referring to an attractive female co-worker as "a good looker" or a "Number Ten."

No one can ever really define that mysterious property called curb appeal. Yet everybody knows it when they see it.

A residence with curb appeal is a place that most of us consider attractive when we happen to drive past along the street.

Just as many films and television programs establish very unrealistic standards for beauty in this century (not many people in real life resemble high fashion models), the criteria used to assess curb appeal often seem inflated in this era. Many perfectly nice residential properties lack stunning curb appeal.

But if you plan to place your home on the real estate market and you want it to sell quickly, one of the best avenues for focusing your attention involves generating as much curb appeal as possible.

What does this situation mean in practical terms?

Sellers with a discretionary improvement budget may find their dollars going further if they allocate a big portion of the funds to fixing up and beautifying the visible external portions of the residence. This principle holds that money spent trimming the bushes, mowing the lawn, repairing fences, augmenting the front door and planting beautiful trees and flowers will eventually probably come back to you.

To appreciate the full power of curb appeal, just consider this situation: you visit a new town and drive slowly into a middle class neighborhood. Two dwellings gain your immediate attention.

One of the houses you pass maintains a very impressive exterior. With a nicely trimmed front yard, a clean, attractive walkway, pretty flower beds growing in parts of the garden and a well maintained, clean driveway and securely closed garage, it radiates a comfortable, welcoming lifestyle. It stands out in fact *because* it looks so charming from the curbside.

At the opposite end of the same street, you pass an identical home model. It would appear vacant, except for the five cars parked in the driveway and along the lawn. A battered couch sits outside the front door. Long grass grows in the unkempt yard. Tossed soda pop cans and a couple of beer bottles lie abandoned near the curb. And a roaming animal knocked over the trash barrel before the garbage truck arrived and partially dumped its contents across the public sidewalk. The household's uncollected mail bulges from the partly opened mailbox.

Do you hold any doubts about which house you would rather own?

Even if those two houses originally sold for the exact same amount of money when the subdivision developer first offered them to the public, people instinctively know which one will command a higher price on the market today.

I must mention here that I think the curb appeal concept sometimes leads to the application of unfair or at least, uncharitable labels. Our society sometimes makes assumptions for very superficial reasons.

For instance, many senior citizens find keeping up with yard work difficult. Health reasons may distract them from regular maintenance duties, and they may not possess the financial resources to hire lawn care professionals to assist them in managing their residential property. Families mourning the loss of a loved one, people called away to military service, single parents working three jobs and many other folks for a wide variety of reasons, may not maintain a level of curb appeal for their property that their neighbors consider optimal.

But when it comes to placing your residence on the market for the highest possible price, you need to consider maintaining your own curb appeal mandatory. Otherwise you likely won't obtain the attractive purchase offers you would prefer.

Tip #12 Take Time to Smell the Roses

Some real estate professionals recommend that owners placing their properties on the market retain the services of lawn care companies to help them maintain their yards in great condition even during periods of extended absence.

Additionally, planting trees and flowers in strategic places on the grounds of a dwelling may offer potentially big returns in terms of enhancing curb appeal. When people driving past the house notice a spectacular floral display, it may draw their attention away from other issues. They focus on how pretty the yard appears.

For example, home owners with "problem" lawn areas, such as steep hillsides that prove difficult to mow, can sometimes save time and effort by planting the entire slope with a flowering ground cover. These types of natural displays provide attractive scenery. It is sometimes possible to augment this type of area with terraced rock wall gardens, too.

Flowers purchased in cartons or grown from seeds can provide an elegant addition to outdoor decors, at a relatively modest cost. Just like skilled craftsmen, talented gardeners sometimes possess an advantage in terms of property improvement. Homeowners who love to garden can often significantly enhance the curb appeal of a residence in this way.

Generally, condominium or homeowner's association groups hire building property management firms. These companies may handle the "curb appeal" of jointly owned buildings. An individual property owner in one of these communities may face limited options in terms of modifying landscaping. However, in this situation, some property owners invest in container gardens for patios and decks as one way to make their own units distinctive.

If you own a large yard, and especially if you reside in a semi-urban area, adding a fruit orchard and some berry bushes to your garden can offer a significant home selling point at a future date. Nut trees may also augment property values. Usually, expecting trees to enhance your property's curb appeal during a sale requires some advance planning, since trees generally require several years of growth before they begin contributing significantly to the appearance of the property.

Residents of warmer states in particular may find that their ability to grow attractive garden plants around the home for several months improves their property's attractiveness. Flowering trees and bushes can lend some especially charming accents to outdoor environments. They may attract song birds to the yard. During seasons when the blossoms bloom, these types of plants can literally transform a home's surroundings with vibrant bursts of natural color.

One useful step that homeowners can take well in advance of placing a property on the market involves obtaining a software program to demonstrate how the house and grounds will appear a few years down he road. If you wonder whether or not you should add a particular tree to a certain location, these types of programs can serve as useful visualization tools.

You can input the specific dimensions of your house and grounds and project the growth of trees, bushes and flowers based on average growth patterns. By using a computer program of this type, it may be possible to determine the best location for adding new plants. You can obtain a realistic image of what the property will look like ten, 15 or even 20 years in the future. Sierra Software produces excellent, inexpensive gardening programs of this nature, including "Complete Land Designer," and there are many other similar products on the market, as well.

Tip #13: Advice

Many professionals in industries that offer frequent home improvement services provide free advice to home owners interested in making property improvements. If you find yourself considering placing residential property on the market in the near future, but want to obtain creative ideas for beautifying the house first, and you happen to reside near a large urban or suburban area, you may find many free seminars and brief workshops offered by local businesses.

For instance, some home building stores will provide informational seminars to prospective customers during weekend hours about various home projects. Often these types of presentations include brief demonstrations and, of course, a sales pitch to purchase specific product lines carried by the retailer. It can be quite educational to attend these sessions to gain general knowledge about the types of products and services available.

For example, you might learn useful tips for replacing kitchen tiles, building garden fences or constructing cement pathways. Although many people have a tendency to discount brief retailer demonstrations as mainly commercial in nature, even people who eventually elect not to buy particular upgrades may gain a better appreciation for the costs of a variety of home and yard improvements.

Sometimes community colleges or civic groups will offer longer and more detailed workshops addressing specific real estate enhancement projects, also. These organizations generally charge a fee for attendance, but offer copious information.

These sources can furnish helpful resources to help you develop an appreciation for the types of artisanship involved in certain home improvements. If you ever do need to hire a contractor to perform work on your house, it may enable you to better assess the requirements of the job.

During warmer months, when many contractors work on home building contracts, people in rural areas in particular may encounter difficulty locating craftsmen willing to commute to their remote areas to complete some work. Even city residents frequently encounter slower response times during this period of the year. So if you plan on improving your residence before placing it on the market, it can prove helpful to allow a longer period of time for the completion of certain assignments during late spring, summer and early fall months and to anticipate an even lengthier time frame for the completion of work on subcontracted rural properties. Of course, exceptions exist. But planning ahead for these types of delays can save stress.

Tip #14: Keep Tabs on Local Homeowner Association Requirements

My late husband made a point of attending homeowner association meetings whenever possible. Many of these types of local regulatory bodies enforce requirements that ultimately impact a property owner's real estate very significantly. Usually homeowner's associations behave in a reasonable way, but you may occasionally find a Board that gets carried away with its own authority, or one that fails to implement rules.

Before a property owner places a home on the real estate market in a development governed by a homeowner association (HOA), it makes sense to check with the Board about any regulations pertaining to lawns and building exteriors. For instance, sometimes a property owner may find it imperative to follow quite specific landscaping guidelines designed to maintain the unified appearance of the development.

Checking first if you plan on adding a semi-permanent structure, such as a pergola or picnic table to your yard, can save disappointment later.

And since HOAs vary widely in the level of participation and interest, property owners who make a point of attending meetings can also avoid surprises. Attendance can help keep you well informed about what is going on in your neighborhood. When a rule impacts your plans for beautifying your residence, you will be the first to know about the situation.

For example, the condominium complex where my husband had maintained a unit for many years on Lake Tahoe, at one point developed a serious concern about bears roaming loose on the property. Even though it was gated and enclosed by a high fence, bears one summer began descending from the nearby mountains and raiding garbage containers on the premises at dusk. The association in charge of the development urged residents to take specific steps in handling garbage disposal to try and reduce the problem of nocturnal bear visits. My husband cared deeply about wildlife; he valued the well being of people in the area, but he also cared about the local bear population, too, and hoped that people would take steps to avoid attracting bear visits.

So, depending on your specific situation, you may find HOAs able to furnish information about a wide array of topics impacting your neighborhood. One function that many of these organizations perform involves trying to maintain curbside appeal for everyone in the community. While the subdivision rules controlling the modifications that can occur in some residential communities to individual properties may involve a lot of details, these regulations do stem ultimately from a shared community goal of maintaining property values.

Tip # 15: Unsheltered Vehicles

As much as possible while preparing your home for the real estate market, try and find ways to reduce the number of vehicles parked in the driveway and along the street outside your home. If you lack a garage, it may not be possible to completely eliminate parked cars outside the premises. But storing them securely in a garage at night, and minimizing parking volume along the street to the extent possible, will allow prospective buyers to better visualize your residence.

Sometimes home owners contemplating relocation can temporarily store excess vehicles at lots in campgrounds, RV parks or storage units. If a member of the family enjoys working on these machines as a hobby, it might even be possible to rent a small garage as a storage-and-tool shop. This expenditure can make sense by helping to beautify the driveway and also reduce the visible property of the home owner.

You want prospective buyers to imagine **their** vehicles, boats and bicycles parked nearby- **not yours**. So take the short term measure of removing as many visible items of transportation as possible ahead of placing your home on the market.

Tip#16: On Top of Things

In enhancing the curb appeal, a property owner must consider the exterior of the home from top to bottom. For instance, if someone expends a lot of time and effort beautifying the lawn and front entrance, but asphalt shingles overhead appear dirty, moss-covered and curling, the roof's poor condition may steal a visitor's attention away from otherwise attractive features of the home.

Sometimes some fairly simple steps can correct this situation, especially if a roof remains structurally sound and does not leak. Other times the problem of an unattractive but still functional roof remains difficult to resolve. It really depends on the individual circumstance. Here are some steps you can take:

First, if you have an open gutter to collect rain and melting snow from the roof running along the rim of the roof or under the eaves and you have not already done so, you may want to consider clearing out the debris inside. Over time, mud and fallen leaves can accumulate in this location in cold climates, impairing the effectiveness of the roof's runoff systems. This in turn may clog and causing splatter to stain the home's exterior. So periodically cleaning out the gutters can help keep the house's exterior surfaces looking much cleaner.

Second, if you are in doubt about the condition of the roof, ask a roofing professional whose opinion you trust to evaluate it for you. You may discover the roof maintains an excellent condition. On the other hand, it may require a good cleaning instead, or even a replacement or partial replacement.

The type of roofing covering the dwelling may significantly impact this situation. Today, metal roofing has become increasingly common. Metal roofs may consist of large sheets of colorized metal or metal-cladding, or it may even occur in the form of shingles. Some metal roof shingles at a distance remain nearly indistinguishable in appearance from other materials, such as wooden or asphalt shingles. Fortunately, metal roofs clean more readily than many other types of roof coverings. Check with the manufacturer for specific cleaning directives.

Another widely used roofing material today remains asphalt tile. In order to enhance the protective and fire-retardant properties of this material, some manufacturers reportedly add extra granules to the material to thicken it. This can inadvertently cause problems in some damp climates if algae begin growing on the surface. It is said to occur most frequently in structures surrounded by heavy vegetation and shaded areas. You can recognize this problem by the formation of black streaks along the roof.

Your roofer should be able to clean away this contaminant using a strong brush and an inexpensive bleach or vinegar solution. Some sources recommend power washing as a cleaning method, but reportedly this step can dislodge some asphalt shingles and thus create more problems.

Simply applying the cleaning agent with a non-powered manual spray bottle and then rinsing it the same way can usually clean quickly and with minimal expense. There are also effective commercial roof cleaning agents sold in many home improvement stores. If you have any questions about the best way to clean your specific property exterior, consider checking with your HOA and property insurance agent for clarification.

Taking steps to clean the gutters, roof and exterior in advance of placing the home on the market can sometimes greatly augment curbside appeal. This process does involve varying degrees of expense, depending on the roof, its issues, the cleaning process and the personnel involved.

Tip#17: Doorbells and the Chimes of Money

Today a wide array of doorbell options exist that may allow property owners to replace or repair malfunctioning doorbells without requiring the service of an electrician. If you have any safety concerns about the underlying reason for the malfunction, though, it remains a good idea to ask an electrician to check out the problem.

When your home goes on the market, you will want the doorbell working effectively. Depending on the type of unit, repairing a doorbell can be inexpensive or impose a significant cost.

Most real estate professionals recommend seeking out a doorbell reverberating in a pleasant, neutral way. If you have an offbeat sense of humor, now is not the time to indulge it. Try and provide a clear, accurate, simple chime that does not involve loud music, irritating sounds or anything unusual.

Again, you want callers and visitors who happen to be home buying prospects to be able to visualize their households residing comfortably in your dwelling. Some of them can't do that effectively when a seller insists on extensively personalizing a communication, even in a light hearted, humorous vein.

Tip #18: A Welcoming Entrance

Most household take steps to create an inviting home entrance. If you have not done so already, it makes sense to carefully study the main exterior entrance to the home from the standpoint of a visitor when you work to enhance curbside appeal in anticipation of selling your residence.

The humorist Mark Twain once observed that while everyone *talks* about the weather, but no one every *does* anything about it...

Property owners readying their homes for the market enjoy an opportunity to prove him mistaken by taking steps to overcome inclement weather conditions on their doorstep, at least in a small way. During some times of the year when harsh wind or temperature conditions impact houses in some locations, cleaning the front entrance more frequently may prove helpful. A spic and span front doorway usually makes a favorable first impression on prospective home buyers.

Also, to spruce up the environment, adding a fresh, brand new welcome mat outside the front door may signal a well-maintained clean interior. Some households experience fairly heavy foot traffic in this location. Periodically replacing the outdoor mat can offer a fairly inexpensive way of maintaining a crisp, clean appearance.

Some safety experts recommend that removing trees and shrubbery from the immediate vicinity of entrances and windows provides additional security to residents in a home. In high crime areas, burglars have been known to prowl in obstructed places around houses. So keeping a clear field of vision in these access locations can contribute to home safety and also help promote curbside appeal.

Many homeowners beautify exterior surfaces by applying protective coatings of sealants. These materials are often either epoxy or polyurethane-based. They may enhance the long term life of a surface by offering additional protection from the elements. It might not prove to be a cost-effective home improvement to consider when placing your property on the market, situations vary, but adding these types of coatings to an exterior surface usually assists with long term maintenance.

To enhance the entrances of the house and maximize energy efficiency relatively inexpensively, consider applying extra insulation strips at the base of doorways. This step can help reduce drafts into a home. Some real estate experts also recommend caulking around windows.

One very important point: if you plan on selling your residential real estate in a cold climate during any time of year when snow and sleet pose a transportation hazard, make certain that you arrange a way to maintain ice-free driveways, walks and front entrances.

Tip #19: A Big Splash and Bouncing Balls

If you plan on marketing a home that includes a privately maintained swimming pool, you may need to pay particular attention to a number of curbside appeal issues. Some experts recommend selling a used above ground pool as a preliminary matter and not marketing it with the real estate. The option you take may depend on the age and condition of the pool, the extent to which it remains moveable, and its general appearance and safety features.

Below ground pools also present a number of issues for homeowners. In some communities, having an outdoor swimming pool associated with the residence greatly enhances value.

On the other hand, pools can present a variety of complex issues, too, including potential leaking and repair problems, the cost of maintaining them, the safety of pool drains and pumping equipment and local ordinances concerning gates and barriers and water availability. Today, in many parts of the Southwestern United States, traditionally viewed as a portion of the Sunbelt, concerns about water shortages have lead to efforts to restrict water use. Most of these conservation efforts focus on lawn watering systems. However, in places with hefty water bills, maintaining backyard pools may involve significant regular expenditures.

In some locations, property owners with aging pools eventually stop maintaining them. If the pool remains unfilled, this situation can also impose a potential safety hazard. Recently, some people with older backyard pools have successfully turned them into lily ponds and fish ponds. Fencing these areas usually still remains a wise idea for safety reasons.

Backyard pools appeal to many families in sunny climates. It may be helpful before buying or selling a home with a swimming pool to consult with your attorney to discuss the best course of action for adhering to local pool safety ordinances and to work out a plan for maintaining pool costs effectively.

Similarly, privately owned basketball hoops, volleyball courts or tennis courts also represent additional recreational amenities. Driveway basketball hoops can provide a helpful selling feature, or not (situations vary). It remains prudent to check to make sure that your basketball hoop remains tightly connected to adjoining support materials. If it sustains heavy use, this type of athletic equipment benefits sometimes from a quick brush-up coating of metallic paint on rims and poles.

If an outdoor court is paved with asphalt or concrete, it helps to go over the surface and make sure that it conveys a neat, smooth, well-maintained appearance. Dirt surfaces may benefit from the addition of fresh sand.

Some sources recommend checking the netting on volleyball and tennis courts before placing a home on the market. The net may require cleaning or some repair. Amenities such as backyard pools and courts are appreciated by many purchasers, but they won't necessarily significantly increase the price of a home in many neighborhoods, where they may represent a desirable enhancement but not necessarily command full value upon re-sale.

Tip #20 Painting: Right and Wrong

Another tip for enhancing curb appeal and basic home repairs relates to exterior painting. It can be important to know when (and when not) to pick up a paint brush during a home beautification process.

Sometimes painting a bathroom or other room in the premises selectively will cover superficial scuff and scrape marks and enhance overall appearance. A fresh paint odor can help improve the marketability of some residences. However, extensive repainting proves expensive sometimes. The cost of high quality house paint adds up if a property owner decides to completely paint an interior or exterior.

This issue became complicated a few years ago, when for health and safety reasons prohibitions went into effect on using lead in paint. While lead poses a definite hazard to children who consume peeling lead paint, and it is a serious environmental toxin, the removal of this substance from many exterior paints has also reportedly decreased the typical lifespan of many outdoor paints. Siding possibly became a more popular option for many homeowners as a result of this change.

I can relay the following account because nothing involved in the interaction was confidential. Some details have been changed to protect the privacy of the people involved.

Several years ago, I met a couple who had experienced great difficulty selling their home in a resort community. They were very kind, talented individuals. The house itself should have disappeared from the market quickly; it was a nice property offered at a reasonable price, boasting many attractive features. The couple wanted to sell urgently in order to move overseas.

Both the husband and wife had found their lack of offers distressing. Unfortunately, instead of waiting for their agent to conduct more open houses, they took it upon themselves to improve the residence by re-painting. And instead of following their agent's suggestion that they redecorate in neutral colors, they enthusiastically began covering everything – and I do mean *everything* -- with fresh paint.

The wife preferred violet, and so she painted bedroom walls, closets, hallways, kitchen walls, kitchen cupboards, stair rails, baseboards, bathrooms, living room bookshelves, ceilings and even the pantry in this shade. The Power of Violet captured the instant attention of anyone walking indoors.

Unfortunately, her husband determined that in his opinion the exterior of the home would look much better with fresh paint, too. He transformed a natural pine log exterior into a coal black one, from the roof to the basement window wells. The house sold eventually, but for a considerably reduced price.

The couple in most peoples' opinion did not make a mistake in repainting; they simply erred in choosing colors that they individually preferred. If they had been moving into the home and not trying to sell it, this course of action would have brought them joy. But they learned to their sorrow that the color preferences of buyers, not sellers, should control any repainting when a home goes on the real estate market.

It may help you market your home if you allow your buyers to make their own color choices as much as possible. If you repaint prior to selling, and many people do find this process helpful, try to adopt a *conservative* color scheme. In this context, bland trumps beautiful.

As a general rule of thumb, in my opinion it makes sense to paint interior walls using white paint, to allow wooden interior fixtures to retain a natural wood shade and to never, ever paint exterior walls black. Many buyers hold a strong aversion to black painted home exteriors, perhaps an irrational bias rooted in Halloween lore.

Tip #21 Let There Be Light!

One of the easiest and least expensive ways to improve the marketability of a residence is a task that many people overlook (pun intended). And it remains a very simple tip: make certain all the light bulbs work.

Check every light inside and outside the house, one by one, and remove and clean glass fixtures to eliminate dust and any accumulated dead moths or other insect debris.

By paying some attention to the light fixtures, a homeowner can make certain that prospective buyers will be able to see every nook and cranny of the home more clearly. Additionally, the illumination assists showings that occur during the evening or night time hours, the only periods that some people can view a property.

This tip also concerns an important subtext. By making sure that every light works perfectly, you will convey to visitors that the property has been well cared for and maintained. Psychologists have demonstrated that people who see brightly lit premises tend to remember the area more favorably and in clearer terms than dimly illuminated places. This effect may seem subtle, but it does pay off in terms of making a good impression when a buyer visits the property for the first time.

If as a property owner you have contemplated adding exterior lighting to the home and you can afford to do so conveniently, taking this step prior to placing the residence on the real estate market is not a bad idea. People appreciate exterior lighting, especially if it reduces the chance of a nasty slip or fall. If the home is ever shown at night, it is nice to illuminate the front entrance.

At one time, lighting sometimes cost a considerable sum of money. Today, many options exist in terms of both interior and exterior lighting. Prices for some types of lights have fallen. This kind of upgrade today may prove cost effective.

Tip #22 Relocate Pets in Advance of Showings

To the extent possible, it makes sense to relocate your pet dog, cat, bunny, ferret, iguana, Boa or pocket pet temporarily during a showing of the home. If prospective buyers find it difficult visualizing themselves living in your house when they see your jacket in the closet, just imagine how much trouble some folks have when they encounter Fido romping around the back yard or enclosed in a utility room?

Although many people love pets (I'm in that camp!), the presence of one during a real estate showing detracts attention away from the virtues of the property. In this situation, you want prospective buyers to feel comfortable exploring every room on the premises, plus the yard. They need to see your home in order to consider purchasing it, without worrying that they will meet an overly protective or exuberant animal.

Most veterinary clinics, groomers, trainers and boarding kennels will entertain requests from clients to babysit their pets for a small fee during a real estate showing. If you feel comfortable temporarily relocating a pet off-premises for a brief period of time, it makes sense to take this step in the interest of improving the chance of a sale.

And sometimes pets do not fare especially well during real estate showings, because everyone's attention centers on the property. A co-worker of mine a number of years ago came to work distraught because she could not locate one of her two beloved pets. The cat, a saucy, strong-willed Siamese tomcat, had resided with the family for several years and never missed a meal. But one day he uncharacteristically failed to show up for dinner.

My co-worker searched everywhere in the neighborhood and could not locate him. We all felt very sad when we heard her story because it seemed possible the indoor-outdoor Siamese had encountered an accident along the road. My colleague and her husband were heart sick. They both feared that their old friend had met an untimely demise.

But the answer emerged just a few days later. The one place the couple never considered searching was the vacant house across the street. It was on the real estate market at the time.

It turned out the property had been the site of an open house on the day the cat disappeared. Fortunately, the agent re-visited it about three days later in order to conduct a showing. As soon as the realtor opened the front door-- out ran my co-workers tomcat. He had apparently slipped into the house unnoticed with some visitors and no one had observed him when the premises were locked up at the end of the day.

Tip #23 Clean Up Dirty Tile Grout

Homes with tiled floors and fixtures in bathrooms and kitchens tend to show much better when the home owner takes steps to have dirty tile grout professionally cleaned. Today, chemical bonding processes exist which can essentially restore well worn tiled surfaces to a nearly new, clean appearance.

Since many buyers focus special attention on hygiene in these environments, it can enhance the attractiveness of a property significantly when tile grout displays a renewed, brighter surface.

In many locations, carpet cleaning companies will also perform professional tile cleaning. These services can often assist homeowners in preparing homes for the market. If you do decide to have your carpet professionally cleaned in contemplation of putting the residence on the market, a fairly widespread practice, it may be an ideal time to inquire if the company can also professionally clean and refurbish bathroom and kitchen tiled surfaces.

Tip #24 Rickety Steps Collapse Sales

For centuries, the concept of stairways leading nowhere won attention from artists and architects[1]. Many slapstick humorists make visual jokes about stairways heading towards abysses. But in real life, nobody wants to encounter one of these unfunny disasters.

Let me digress for just a moment.

When I attended the veterinary program, during the third year, I received permission to foster a blood donor dog named Franz. He was a big, black Greyhound (with some Doberman pinscher in his bloodline) who evidently had not enjoyed a lot of contact with people during his previous existence. He adjusted to life around human beings with some difficulty.

Greyhounds donated to veterinary programs frequently do not survive long. However, the administration at the college I attended did direct some of them into specialized services that provided them with adoption opportunities. One was the blood donor program. It permitted dogs and cats to supply blood for transfusions. Students could keep the dogs with them during the course of their attendance at the school, while the donors supplied periodic blood donations for the benefit of the animal patients undergoing surgery and critical care at the Teaching Hospital; upon graduation, the students then furnished permanent homes to the animals in their care. It was a win-win idea.

In Franz' case, he seemed to enjoy living at home as a pet, but getting used to a domestic setting required a lot of adjustment for him. He had spent his entire life up to that point in kennels.

---

[1] http://gizmodo.com/5976107/22-stairways-that-lead-nowhere

The house had a family den located on the second level, a room accessed via a long, steep enclosed staircase leading into the finished basement. The staircase ended in front of a bare white wall and it was necessary to turn the corner at the bottom of the stairs to access the den, which could not be seen at all from the stairway.

Greyhounds as large dogs usually require practice to learn how to navigate stairs. Poor Franz had very limited experience with steps. He hesitated to venture down into the den. When the rest of the household gathered downstairs, he wanted to join us. But for several weeks, the stairs presented too significant a barrier for him. He would sit at the top whining, afraid to make the downward journey.

I worked to teach him to go up and down stairs, without success. Then one day, I sat on the top step and closely watched one of my other dogs walking toward the den. Upon reaching the bottom and turning the corner, she appeared to literally disappear from sight at that angle of vision. This event shocked me. I must have seen people and animals heading into the den hundreds of times previously, but I had never appreciated that from the vantage point of the top step they appeared to vanish into thin air once they reached the bottom and turned the corner.

Franz eventually learned to go downstairs and after the first successful trip, he tackled the stairs with gusto. To this day, I wonder whether it was the prospect of disappearing into the unknown at the bottom of that particular stairway rather than the awkward incline for a big dog that generated his initial anxiety. With his keen sense of smell, Franz would have been aware that people and dogs had traveled elsewhere in the lower level of the house, but he would not have been able to know their situation until he ventured into the basement himself.

But to return more directly to the topic of steps:

In advance of any home showing, a real estate owner can usually improve the appearance and safety of a property by making sure that all exterior (and interior) steps remain solid and secure. Rickety steps can collapse sales.

Today, many home improvement stores sell sets of steps for staircases. Employees in these establishments will provide excellent advice about installing secure, safe steps or locating qualified contractors to complete that task. There are also some companies marketing pre-formed metal steps, not to mention firms that will supply homeowners with very solid concrete ones applied directly on the premises using molds.

Houses constructed on elevated slabs, or those with old basements and storm shelters, may require special attention to rickety steps. No one wants to trip while looking at a residence, including the owner. If repairing a weak step is a task you plan on completing at some point anyway, why not make certain the issue gets addressed before placing a home on the market?

Replacing faulty steps with safe, secure ones offers greater peace of mind to everyone involved in a real estate transaction. Carpeting over rickety steps will not solve the problem, and may sometimes make it worse, by causing visitors to proceed without the extra caution they would probably demonstrate if the stairs did not appear superficially secure.

Tip #25 When Rails Matter

In addition to making sure that steps on your property remain functional, investing in handrails to provide additional support can prove useful. This issue becomes especially important when dealing with steeply sloping stairs.

Some properties maintain very steep Victorian Era style- staircases. Even when these remain quite secure, people attempting to navigate up or down high, sharply angled stairs may encounter problems without a sturdy handrail to offer additional support. Elderly or infirm visitors to home showings in particular may encounter difficulty climbing up and down these types of stairways.

Nobody conducting an open house or showing visitors through a home can be certain how well their guests will navigate stairs inclining at sharp angles. To help prevent falls, installing a sturdy handrail can supply a much better solution than hoping that serious injuries won't result if someone trips.

Tip #26 Through a Glass, Clearly

Another simple measure to improve the appearance of your home during a showing involves cleaning all the windows in the home. Many people do this on a regular basis anyway. However, in some busy families, or in households with a lot of elevated windows, the cleaning of some of these structures may get postponed repeatedly.

Make an effort to clean these hard to access surfaces before a showing. Simply washing them with warm, soapy water, then rinsing with a squeegee can massively amplify the amount of light entering a dwelling. This situation may allow prospective buyers to visualize the home better.

Cleaning windows proves an especial challenge in some places with high levels of air pollution. For instance, a newscast reportedly recently that Beijing in the Peoples Republic of China sustained 175 days in 2014 of air quality conditions so poor that people suffering from health conditions could not even venture outdoors safely. Photographs of the city during this period show a thick, soupy black mist hanging visibly in the air. Just imagine how difficult cleaning the exterior surfaces of windows would be under those difficult environmental conditions?[2]

To reach very high windows, popular in some home models, an extendable cleaning brush can serve as a useful tool. By using a long extendable brush, it may be possible to avoid having to go up and down ladders carrying soapy water. Most modern home supply stores sell these types of devices.

Some home owners may also have access to robotic cleaning tools that can scale heights to clean glass surfaces. Once again, these labor saving measures offer convenience to property owners.

---

[2] *See* http://www.npr.org/blogs/parallels.2015/03/04/390689033/the-anti-pollution-documentary-thats-taken-china-by-storm. Millions of people in China share a deep concern about the issue of achieving clean air targets.

Tip #27 Mirrors and Reflection

To expand the appearance of space within a home, some builders affix mirrors to closet doors and interior walls. This can prove to be an expensive form of decoration, but also creates an impression of expanded space. Many trailer homes utilize mirrors in decor extensively for this reason.

If your home or apartment contains an unusually narrow room layout, you might find it helpful to install mirrors over some surfaces to increase the sensation of free space. This strategy proves especially beneficial if light from a window enters the location, to be reflected in the mirror.

If you do add mirrors to the environment to create a sense of greater space in a small or unusually configured room in the home, it remains important to clean the surface of the mirror before a home showing. Smudges or streaks can impede the desired effect.

Tip #28 A Fuming Problem: Smokers and Non-Smokers

One issue that may arise when a home is place on the market concerns odors lingering in a dwelling occupied by smokers. People who regularly use tobacco products sometimes do not appreciate the extent to which cigarette, pipe and cigar fumes cling to surfaces in the home.

My father used to smoke tobacco cigarettes daily. I rarely noticed the odor of cigarettes lingering in public places, on clothing or around the home during childhood. My father would regard people critical of smoking as overly sensitive types, and he tended to dismiss their complaints about second hand smoke out of hand.

After my father died, and the family home became non-smoking, my sensitivity to cigarette fumes naturally increased. Today, I can smell someone's tobacco smoke across a restaurant from a long distance away. My father would never have believed it possible.

Smokers do not possess the olfactory sensitivity to smoking odors that non-smokers take for granted. This can pose problems for them when they place real estate on the market. The strong tobacco nicotine odor that pervades drapes, furniture and other items in the home does not usually reach their awareness and it may hamper their ability to market a property to non-smokers.

Some real estate professionals advise smokers to retain carpet cleaning companies to conduct a thorough cleaning of premises before placing their homes on the market. This step will not remove cigarette odors if a smoker still resides in the house, however. This phenomenon may be one reason why some hotels dedicate specific rooms as either smoking or non-smoking.

Tip #29 Cat Odor and Pet Issues

I am certain that pet owners remain largely unaware of the distinctive aroma of dogs and cats living on premises also. Since I reside with a number of pets, I am a very poor judge indeed of this condition,

When I worked at Wheeler Realty, the firm took periodic "house tours" so that all of the sales agents in the office could walk through listings and hopefully contribute to finding buyers for these properties. It was a wonderful opportunity to gain familiarity with many aspects of real estate. Although participating in these excursions remained optional, I noticed that the most successful agents and brokers in the office always chose to attend the tours whenever possible. They wanted to be aware of the features of available properties.

There were agents in the office who could literally walk in the front door of a residential property for the first time and know with assurance whether the occupants had ever kept a pet cat on the premises during the last decade. Reportedly, cats possess a very unique, but distinctive, odor.

Some property buyers view pet smells in much the same way that nonsmokers often regard smoking odors. It can be a big turn-off to some prospective purchasers, although large numbers of people cannot detect these odors very effectively.

If you do own pets, it may assist your house marketing efforts to thoroughly clean carpets, upholstery and other furnishings before offering the residence for sale. Additionally, it helps to patrol the yard daily with a pooper scooper while the home remains on the market.

On the plus side, if you have invested in permanent pet kennels or sturdy pet fencing during your stay in the home, these items may be viewed as positive features by many prospective buyers with pets.

Tip #30 The Remarkable Power of Cinnamon

Some real estate agents contend that an extremely helpful technique for anyone holding a real estate showing may involve boiling a couple of cinnamon sticks in water on the stove in the kitchen about fifteen minutes beforehand. You want a strong aroma of fresh, warm cinnamon to pervade the kitchen area, if at all possible.

People reportedly do respond with great sensitivity to odors in their immediate environment. Some studies have shown that the majority of folks appreciate the smell of freshly baked cinnamon rolls (this odor is even considered sexy by many men).

Possibly cinnamon aromas infusing the kitchen provide a favorable environment because they connote a warm element of domesticity. People can enter the room and visualize themselves baking and using the kitchen or consuming food at the table. The use of cinnamon may prove helpful in assisting marketing efforts in properties occupied by smokers and pet owners.

Conclusion

Hopefully, some of these tips will benefit you if you are placing your residence on the real estate market. It can require a lot of hard work and effort to sell real estate successfully. Good luck with preparing your home for the real estate market and I hope the points raised in this brief book will prove helpful!

www.ingramcontent.com/pod-product-compliance
Lightning Source LLC
Chambersburg PA
CBHW071004180526
45168CB00003B/1282